FORECAST!NG

BILL McAULIFFE

WEATHER X BOOKS

CREATIVE EDUCATION · CREATIVE PAPERBACKS

FORE

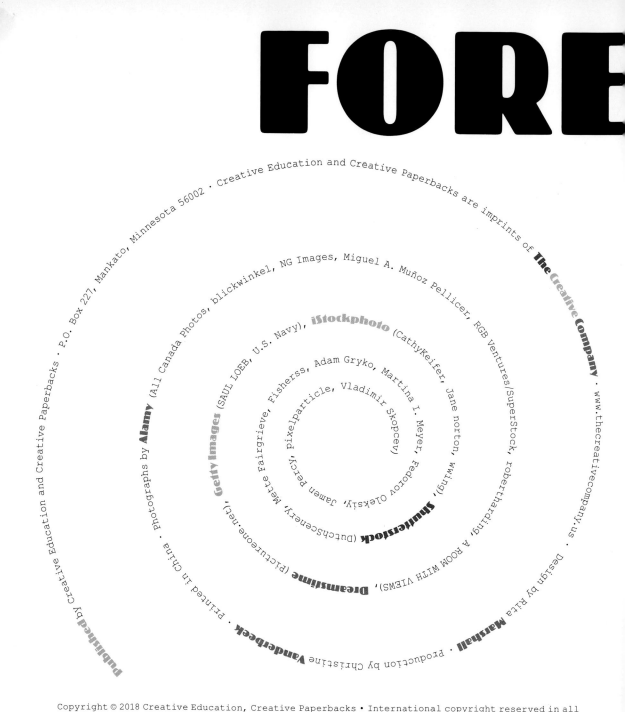

Published by Creative Education and Creative Paperbacks · P.O. Box 227, Mankato, Minnesota 56002 · Creative Education and Creative Paperbacks are imprints of The Creative Company · www.thecreativecompany.us · Design by Rita Marshall · Production by Christine Vanderbeek · Printed in China · Photographs by Alamy (All Canada Photos, blickwinkel, NG Images, Miguel A. Muñoz Pellicer, RGB Ventures/SuperStock, roberthardingg, A ROOM WITH VIEWS), Dreamstime (Dutchscenery), Getty Images (SAUL LOEB, U.S. Navy), iStockphoto (CathyKeifer, Jane norton, wwing), Shutterstock (Dutchscenery, Mette Fairgrieve, Fisherss, Adam Gryko, Martina I. Meyer, Fedorov Oleksiy, Vladimir Skopcev, Jamen percy, pixelparticle), (Pictureone.net)

Library of Congress Cataloging-in-Publication Data • Names: McAuliffe, Bill, author. • Title: Forecasting / Bill McAuliffe. • Series: X-Books: Weather. • Includes bibliographical references and index. Summary: A countdown of five of the most devastating weather-related disasters in which forecasting enabled adequate response provides thrills as readers discover more about this life-saving science. • IDENTIFIERS: LCCN 2016059687/ ISBN 978-1-60818-824-6 (HARDCOVER) / ISBN 978-1-62832-427-3 (PBK) / ISBN 978-1-56660-872-5 (EBOOK) • Subjects: LCSH: Weather forecasting—Juvenile literature. • CLASSIFICATION: LCC QC995.43.M43 2017 / DDC 551.63—dc23 • CCSS: RI.3.1-8; RI.4.1-5, 7; RI.5.1-3, 8; RI.6.1-2, 4, 7; RH.6-8.3-8
First Edition HC 9 8 7 6 5 4 3 2 1 • First Edition PBK 9 8 7 6 5 4 3 2 1

CAST!NG

CONTENTS

WEATHER
X
BOOKS

WEATHER FORECASTING

is telling what weather will
happen in the future based
on available information.

XTRAORDINARY
WEATHER

Predicting the future
is never easy. But
weather forecasters
do it every day.
They use advanced
technology and math.
They use special
equipment and
computers, too. And
sometimes, they use
their own gut feeling.

Forecasting Basics

Weather on Earth is always changing. In most places,
it won't stay the same for long. Warm or cold, wet or
dry, windy or calm. Clashes between these conditions
are what make weather.

Earth warms under the sun each day. At night, it
cools. When warm and cool air meet, water droplets
form. They often fall to the ground as rain or snow.
Meanwhile, changes in **air pressure** cause wind. Wind
pushes warm and cold air around. That sets the stage
for cloudy or sunny weather.

EXOSPHERE above 375 miles (604 km)

THERMOSPHERE 53 to 375 miles (85.3–604 km) high

MESOSPHERE 31 to 53 miles (49.9–85.3 km) high

STRATOSPHERE 10 to 31 miles (16.1–49.9km) high

TROPOSPHERE 0–10 miles (0–16.1 km) high

EARTH'S ATMOSPHERE

The atmosphere is the air that surrounds and is bound to Earth. It regulates temperatures. It makes life on Earth possible. The atmosphere is made up of several layers.

MOST WEATHER occurs in the troposphere.

AIRPLANES FLY in the lower stratosphere.

MOST METEORS burn up in the mesosphere.

THE INTERNATIONAL SPACE STATION orbits in the thermosphere.

Man-made satellites take pictures of Earth.

The pictures show how weather systems develop.

They show how the systems move, too.

Satellites help forecasters understand weather.

SATELLITES HELP CIRCLE EARTH

Forecasters study math and science. They examine maps. They look at weather in other places. Satellites give them a wide view of weather on Earth. Computers calculate possible forecasts. Sometimes, forecasters rely on experience. They think about what happened last time conditions were similar. All of this helps forecasters figure out what weather might be on the way.

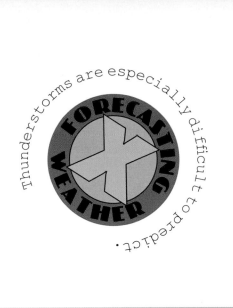

Thunderstorms are especially difficult to predict.

FORECASTING WEATHER

Forecasts of daily temperatures and precipitation are challenging to make. They are reliable only a few days from the present.

Xtreme Forecasting Tool #5

Mathematics In the early 1900s, Norwegian scientist Jacob Bjerknes suggested that weather might be predicted using math. But a single forecast would require thousands of repeated measurements and calculations. Computers were the answer. The first weather forecast by a computer occurred in 1950. It took 24 hours to calculate what the weather would be like in another 24 hours. Today, such forecasts are done in seconds.

In 1922, the first test of math-based forecasting failed to "predict" weather that had already happened.

Forecasting Factors

People pay attention to weather close to the ground. That's where they live, work, and play. Weather can affect their daily plans. Weather happens throughout the atmosphere. Most of it occurs in the lowest layer, though. There, forces push and pull each other. They lift up and press down. Many forecasters describe it as chaotic.

Mathematician Edward Lorenz was the first to put his finger on this chaos. In 1976, he stated that tiny changes in the atmosphere can build up to massive differences. Those changes cause errors in the calculations used to predict weather. He wrote a paper titled "Predictability: Does the Flap of a Butterfly's Wings in Brazil Set Off a Tornado in Texas?" His idea became known as the butterfly effect. It explains how a small change in conditions can greatly disrupt weather. This is why making accurate forecasts is so difficult.

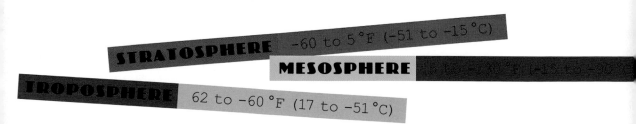

STRATOSPHERE −60 to 5°F (−51 to −15°C)

MESOSPHERE 5 to −130°F (−15 to −90°C)

TROPOSPHERE 62 to −60°F (17 to −51°C)

THERMOSPHERE   −130 to 3,600 °F (−90 to 1,982 °C)

EXOSPHERE   atmosphere fades into outer space

FORECASTING FACTORS FACT

Long-distance weather relationships called teleconnections can cause droughts and storms far from where they begin.

Xtreme Forecasting
Tool #4

The Barometer may have been the first instrument used to understand weather. Italian scientist Evangelista Torricelli was an assistant to Galileo. In the 1640s, he discovered that the level of **mercury** in a tube changed from day to day. He realized this was related to changes in air pressure. Those changes corresponded with changes in the weather. Increasing pressure meant fair weather. Decreasing pressure meant storms.

XASPERATING CHANGES

The weather changes much more rapidly in some places than others. Such changes keep forecasters busy making revisions.

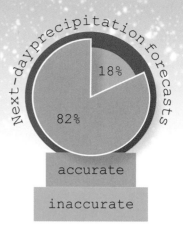

Next-day precipitation forecasts

18%

82%

accurate

inaccurate

FORECASTING CHALLENGES FACT

The most extreme temperature change in Canada was at Pincher Creek, Alberta, in 1962. The temperature rose from −2 to 72 °F (−19 to 22 °C) in an hour.

Outlooks estimate conditions 8 or more days ahead.

WEATHER OUTLOOKS X

Forecasting Challenges

Certain factors can make forecasting weather more
or less difficult. Ocean temperatures change very
slowly. So places close to the seas typically have
more consistent weather. Places far from oceans get
both hotter and cooler. Sometimes these changes
occur quickly. This is particularly true in deserts.
Far from the **equator,** the length of daylight changes
dramatically from month to month. Wide temperature
swings happen almost every day.

Such temperature changes are also common along
the eastern side of North America's Rocky Mountains.
Air rushes up over the mountains. It flies down the other
side to the Great Plains. As the air races downward, it
can warm quickly. Residents of Spearfish, South Dakota,
experienced this in the extreme on January 22, 1943.
The temperature rose from -4 to 45 °F (-20 to 7 °C) in
just 2 minutes! That set a world record.

XTENSIVE PROGRESS

Weather forecasting and warnings go hand in hand. Centuries ago, they were common sayings and rhymes. Today, they have progressed to instant alerts on smartphones.

The telegraph was invented in the 1830s. It allowed people to alert others of approaching weather.

XTENSIVE PROGRESS FACT

In the 1880s, Canadian railroads attached signs with one-word forecasts to trains. These told people what kind of weather was coming.

Long ago, a rhyme helped people prepare for changes in the weather:

Red sky at night, sailor's delight.

Red sky at morning, sailor's warning.

The saying was based on observations. Weather tends to move from west to east. And the color of the sky is caused by sunlight reacting with the atmosphere. People didn't realize that the colors they saw had to do with air pressure or the atmosphere. But their understanding of weather got better with time.

In 1743, Benjamin Franklin realized that storms moved from place to place. It was a new idea. But the idea wasn't very useful by itself. People needed to get information *before* the weather changed. A century later, the telegraph made that possible.

In 1854, the British Meteorological Office (or Met Office) began collecting weather data. Met Office founder Robert FitzRoy then developed the world's first national weather forecast and warning system. The United States soon established its own system.

Xtreme Forecasting Tool #3

Drones Unmanned aircraft are also known
as drones. Drones are becoming major
players in weather forecasting. They can
collect data in levels of the atmosphere
that balloons only pass through. They can
fly places airplanes cannot reach. And
they are much cheaper. They don't put a
pilot at risk, either. Drones began flying
over hurricanes to collect data in 2010.
Some researchers have even tried flying
them into tornadoes.

XCEPTIONAL FORECASTING

Weather forecasts and warnings are available from many sources. Some private companies track weather. They offer forecasts for sports teams, farmers, and others. Governments provide forecasts, too. How do you pick one?

Forecasting Accuracy

Forecasts get increasingly inaccurate the farther they look into the future. But they are improving. Five- and six-day temperature forecasts in 2012 were as accurate as three- and four-day forecasts in 1992. In stormy weather, precipitation predictions made two days ahead in 2012 were as accurate as one-day forecasts in 2006.

Many people in the U.S. rely on forecasts by the National Weather Service (NWS). There are also hundreds of private forecasting businesses. Several base their forecasts off those made by the NWS. The number of forecasters in the U.S. is expected to rise rapidly in the near future.

COLDEST RECORDED TEMPERATURE IN NORTH AMERICA

Snag, Yukon, Canada   -81 °F (-63 °C) on February 3, 1947

HOTTEST RECORDED TEMPERATURE IN NORTH AMERICA

Death Valley, California   134 °F (57 °C) on July 10, 1913

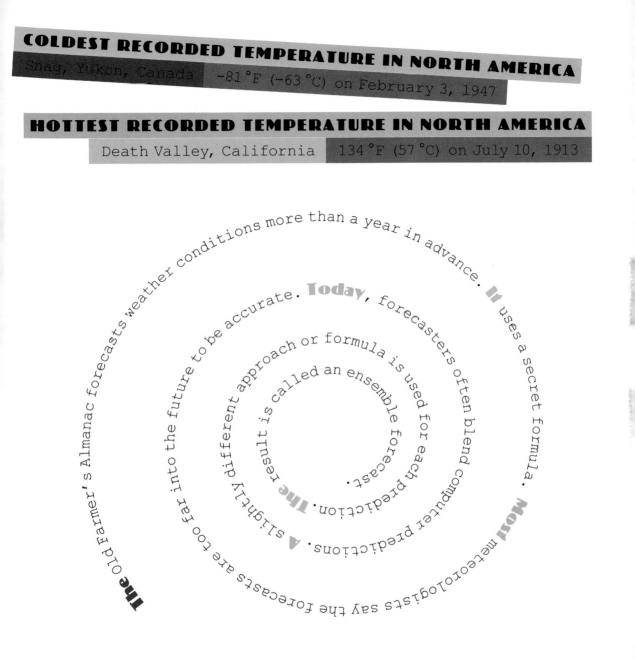

The Old Farmer's Almanac forecasts weather conditions more than a year in advance. It uses a secret formula. Most meteorologists say the forecasts are too far into the future to be accurate. Today, forecasters often blend computer predictions. A slightly different approach or formula is used for each prediction. The result is called an ensemble forecast.

FORECASTING ACCURACY FACT

Forecasts for large areas are less accurate than those for small areas.

ven local forecasts are not considered reliable more than eight days ahead.

Xtreme Forecasting Tool #2

Radar was invented in 1904. This technology was first used to detect warplanes. It could tell a plane's speed and direction. Later, radar's ability to see rain and hail made it a key forecasting tool. Meteorologists found that Doppler radar can measure how fast rain is moving both toward and away from a location. Doppler radar can show when a storm is rotating, too. That motion could produce a tornado.

The aurora borealis (Northern Lights) and aurora australis (Southern Lights) occur within the thermosphere.

The first pictures of Earth from a weather satellite were delivered by the TIROS-1 in 1960.

Robert FitzRoy is known as the "Father of Forecasting."

The Zuni Indians of the southwestern U.S. understood that when the hair on enemies' scalps became damp, rain was on the way.

Researchers attach devices to fish to measure ocean temperatures. This could help predict hurricanes.

Observing animal behavior has long been a non-scientific way to forecast weather.

A radiosonde is an instrument carried into the atmosphere by balloons. It sends weather readings back to meteorologists by radio.

The Met Office's four-day forecasts are now as accurate as its one-day forecasts were in 1980.

Earth's rotation sends air masses spinning in giant pinwheel motions. Weather systems follow these curved paths.

The Greek philosopher Aristotle studied weather more than 2,000 years ago.

In the 1850s, the Smithsonian Institution's director, Joseph Henry, developed daily national weather maps based on telegraph reports.

World War II pilots discovered the jet stream. These strong, high-altitude winds move weather systems around the globe.

Researchers discovered the hook echo in 1954. This radar image is now used to trigger tornado warnings.

Satellites can show

urricanes developing. They can track ash plumes from volcanoes and measure the melting of ice and snow.

Xtreme
Forecasting Tool #1

Helium Balloons In the late 1700s, French
scientists began using **helium** balloons
to travel high into the sky. They measured
temperature and air pressure. They began
to learn how conditions above the ground
affect weather. High up, it was cold.
There was little oxygen. Some of the early
balloonists died. But balloons remain
an essential forecasting tool. Weather
balloons are still launched twice a day
from 800 locations around the world.

GLOSSARY

air pressure – the force or weight of air over a particular location

equator – the imaginary line around the center of the globe, halfway between the North and South poles

helium – an odorless, colorless gas that is lighter than air

mercury – a heavy metallic liquid that rapidly expands or contracts in response to changes in temperature

RESOURCES

Hodgson, Michael. *Basic Essentials of Weather Forecasting*. 2nd ed. Guilford, Conn.: Globe Pequot Press, 1999.

Lynch, John. *The Weather*. Buffalo, N.Y.: Firefly Books, 2002.

Monmonier, Mark. *Air Apparent: How Meteorologists Learned to Map, Predict, and Dramatize Weather*. Chicago: University of Chicago, 1999.

National Oceanic and Atmospheric Administration. Satellite and Information Services. "Imagery and Data." http://www.nesdis .noaa.gov/imagery _ data.html.

INDEX

We have Robert FitzRoy to thank for the term "weather forecasting."